for Sean Virgo

'There is no survivor, there is no future,
there is no life to be created in this form again.
We are looking upon the uttermost finality
which can be written, glimpsing the darkness
which will not know another ray of light.
We are in touch with the reality of extinction.'

H.B. Hough

Book One

The Lost

LAST RITES

Bali Tiger—1937

The little prince of tigers
is dead

The chime of temple bells
An army of votive arrows is offered
A long rope of prayer tethers the sun

Master of the emerald forest
Lord of the crystal waterfall
that feeds the sacred lake
Dread foe of the Monkey King
and the Dragon Master

He was like a flame in the forest
His fearful laughter was in the land

Now he is the small flickering light
of an altar candle
The yellow tallow of memory
slowly flowing away

THE EXCAVATION

Giant Moa—1850

The earth is pulled up
like a coffin lid
Bones like unstrung bows
and a battlefield of broken spearshafts
Giant shin bones cracked
like diviners' yarrow stalks
Beaks like shattered spearheads
The hexagrams of this dry graveyard swamp

I saw the broad clawed footprint
of the giant bird in clay
beneath the hump of the hill
that shadows the valley

Later we found
a ring of Moa skulls
with a hunched chieftain's skeleton
at its centre

Clutched in his spidery grip:
a great Moa egg
like the dragon pearl
that is the Maori moon

Sap of the veronica wood
they called 'Moa's blood'
They roasted Moa flesh on its fires
When an enemy was defiant at the death
they called him 'fierce as the Moa'

And when the white man came
and the Maoris fell
When pestilence and war broke them
And all their world was ending
They cried out 'Ka ngaro i te ngaro a te Moa'
Alas, we are 'lost as the Moa is lost'

In this valley I am shaken
by a vision rising
like the dragon pearl moon
Eclipsing, for a dark hour
the bright noonday sun

SIREN SONG

Steller's Sea Cow—1768

Some still nights
on the shores of Bering's sea
you may imagine them

Huge as the hull
of an overturned ship
Moaning in the rolling surf

Fountain of hot blood pulsing
Furnace of the deep heart
Wave-worn giants, idle lovers
on the swell of the sea

Bigger than elephants
Skin like the bark of an ancient oak
Snorting like horses
Pawing the kelp meadows
with their tough hooves
like bulls in pasture

Tide riders, storm biders
Slow to lust as elephants
Passionate as whales

Beauty here in a thing not itself beautiful
As delight in the play of light
on a mountain or a great rock
Yet something vastly alive
As these once were alive

Some still nights
on the shores of Bering's sea
you may imagine them

the great breath-song
through the sighing night

THE TEMPLE

Barbary Lion—1920

At the gate was the god of Lions
cut in a single massive stone
and raised above the desert sand

In the time of empires
this Lion's eye was a brilliant swastika
A sunwheel on the desert wind
His voice was a stone
rolling over the roof of the world

Even the great parapet of his head
is broken now
The foundation of the temple
is cracked and wasted

Upon the wall
the carved images are all but gone:

vanished men pursue vanished beasts
in that ancient dream of a green
and fruitful land

TAURUS

Aurochs—1740

The last black bull's wounding
was like the bursting
of an old sun in the belly
His roar betrayed the centuries
of refusing to tread warily in this world
Flutes were made from his bones
They play them even now
And hunting horns from his ivory crown

In his veins the singing of a hundred
rapacious birds
He was strength without malice
His forehead was a crushing millstone

Fearful, lordly beast of all the mythologies
Father of the minotaur
A small part of his stubborn blood
is yet in the fighting bulls of the ring
who break the bodies of horses and men

His legend is as ancient as the pale moon
But his life now is only a fish's song
And his spirit is steel and flint striking
on a dark and empty plain

THE CENTAURS

Tarpan—1887

Little wild horses of the steppes
Straggling tribal men
What has the Emperor
behind the Great Wall to fear?
He feeds on peacock tongues
His people cover the lands of the world
His power changes the course of rivers
and shapes the face of the earth

He is disturbed by a terrible vision
He fears the image of a demon
with eight limbs
that is fierce and swift

The Tartar horn blows
and the vision
in a whirlwind comes

At the Dragon Gate
At the Ivory Gate
the bowmen mount the towers
But the demons pass by, not against the wall
but around, their brave hearts pounding distance away

It is the frenzy of the little horses
and the savage tribal men
Two creatures made one

The Tartar horn blows
and the Tarpan carries the tribesmen on
The wall is left to the westwind
The yellow axes of the Imperial Guard are untried
The horsemen pass by, pass around
The cities are pyres
The jade images are shattered
The silk of the Imperial banners
lay tattered beneath the conqueror's hooves

THE HOWLING GOD

Japanese Wolf—1905

Broken wolf's tooth
a charm, set in pounded gold
Ancient blood in a bronze bowl

Shogun hunted Shamanu, the little wolf,
through forests and stony fields
Horses and dogs chased him to mountains
beneath exhausted stars

In ancient days
legend gave him hypnotic power
Geese swooned before
the glowing of his eyes
Beneath the willow tree
travellers and pale maidens
succumbed to his voice

Shamanu, the little Howling God,
ascends the Nine Heavens
Wanders the land of nine jade rivers
and nine jade mountains

Shamanu's blood is red amber now
His eye is sapphire
His flesh the cinnabar ore
that gives up bright quicksilver
and deadly vapour

LEVIATHAN

Atlantic Grey Whale—1730

Tentacle arms reach and grasp,
a myriad of sea creatures bind me,
draw me down into darkness

Sound of seabirds panicking
as the torpedo bodies of black ships
rush and pass

I see a man like a white whale
The shark-tooth harpoon
pierces me with his scream

The barrel of the body turning
the undertow, the crosshold of blankets binding

A shaking cold is on me
a fever without heat
Down, deeper darkness, deeper cold,
no end to this....

* * *

The lost garden of the teeming sea
Here was the shape and bulk that dwarfed
the dragon and the dinosaur
that stunned all mankind in its childhood

How much more we understood
when we knew that the flat earth
rested on Leviathan's back

We were children grown wise as fish

THE LAST CURLEW

Eskimo Curlew — 1970

The last blue shadow falls
into deep snow
Descends in that final whiteness

The glacial stillness of mastodons,
winged lizards and
men who were too gentle

Let us dream of other worlds
Once there were unicorns

Book Two

Ravenwood

THE DARK WOOD

This black card is the Sun
This gold card the Raven

Between the two I place a third
It is unknown to you—

    Midway through this life
    You wake in a dark wood

    Here is the wild lament
    of lost souls

It is the trees
shattered and twisted
that cry out

And from each broken limb
the bright blood comes

THE HANGED MAN

'I am one who made my own rooftree my scaffold'
L'Inferno.

I

The early years were silent
The forest
all sides of me dark
Rain throughout my childhood
Pounding

II

When I am twelve I hanged myself. I have the rope burns still. I am telling you what I see during that time. After the hot bite of rope at my neck. After that and the choke and slow strangling. After the dark and the no pain. After that. I see one tall tree on the ridge alone. From the crown to the root it was split: one half green and living, the other half—every branch, every leaf—lighted with flame. So it was all the time I was hanging.

But there was more, much more, I was seeing. I go travelling into the darkland, where before living folk had never been, or maybe only in dreams, and then just some. It was a forest with only narrow trail, here and there. Maybe made by animal. Came after long time walking with no sound to a village of dead men and women, pale-white. They live in deadtown with earth walls round, heaped up like ditch upsidedown. I come to the gate of skulls and the king of the people come to me. There is a price, he says to me. I pay I say to him.

Take his spear and stab me below the rib, and I scream and all the deadpeople out of their houses and to the gate to see red blood drops fall to ground, each one like jewels, like ruby. After a short time, I cover wound with hand. Enough I say, I paid enough. The blood stops. The king gathers jewels and puts them in a wood box.

III

The women suffering most
with their men gone
The men spent on work in the wood
becoming, themselves, silent and dark
The solitary children
closest to the abandoned women

One long winter night a logger's wife
empties her husband's gun into her head
Our neighbour's boy
is found broken by a bull
against a twisted tree

IV

As a bird I went over this place, for I am telling you I am Raven. As a bird I saw all and the thoughts of the dead folk. There was an orchard there by the river where men with shaved heads drown horses in great whirlpools. In the orchard men were hung from the trees and old crippled women in white priestess robes climb ladders and cut the throats of the hanged with silver knives. The black blood fall into bronze bowls.

v

According to the legend—
Huginn is the blackbird of Thought
and Muninn the blackbird of Memory
Each day they fly out
over all the world

And of them, the old folk say
'I fear for Thought,
lest he come not back.
Yet more I fear
Memory's return.'

VI

Now in the house of the king of deadtown. House made with black gravedirt and bones and carved bright demons, red and gold. I am sat down and fed many things. This their trick to weight me down. But even then I had appetites that none would ever fill. Now they bring me more to eat: a pig and four chickens, and the crimson sorceror's fruits. I consume, devour in a moment. They bring more: a bull, two dogs, two barrels of honey wine, many baskets of bread, a slaughtered bear and two men of deadtown. I swallow all.

Still they do not know me, my legend is not born. Nobody in this time knows Raven. Yet they are in terror of my appetite. Might I consume them all? Now is the time for the destroyer. They call for the deadtown queen.

VII

Waiting long for a favourable wind, the Norsemen decided on an offering. When the lots were drawn, it fell on the king himself. And so it was decided a mock sacrifice would do well enough on this day. The king took off his iron helm and stood on a tree stump with a calf's intestines looped round his neck and tied to a bent tree limb. The warrior Starkad stood by the king's side with a long wand in his hand.

Then as was required, he thrust his wand at the king, calling out: 'Now I give thee to Odin.' The wand at once became a spear and its iron pierced the king through. The stump fell from under his feet, and the calf's gut became a rope, while the branch of the fir tree shot up and lifted the king among the boughs.

And there, King Vikar died of amazement.

Years ago, near the school house
this scene was acted out by children
A game of hanging
that went wrong

Such a game. I with them
Power over life? love of darkness?
The elements?
Wanting the wind in the trees
A stuttering, retched death

VIII

The king never goes at night with the queen. The king brings men for her bed. This I know. I have seen the orchard of hanged men.

Darkland is not the only place. There are other deadtowns. Worse, below the whirlpool and beneath darkland. More terrible, far more terrible.

I went to the house of the queen, most beautiful of women, ruler of all darkland. And yes, men fear the queen who takes a lover each night, and in her passion becomes a mare, and each night rides her lover down to a terrible death.

But not me. Rode her long, my appetite will never be filled. Broke the night mare. Saved the town.

IX

Women, children, and finally
even the men were too gentle

Shifting from place to place
It was always the same
The forest, the ragged edge of the sea
Winds at night, the winter storms
Uprooting force

X

And after I went out of darkland. And after I thought—I know what should be in the livingland and what should not. And after I made the human race, that were not there before. And after I was still so young, just twelve years. And so don't blame me so much yet.

I learn better things later to do, when I am thirteen. But I am telling you that another time.

THE INITIATE

There are elk tracks
in the fallen snow
These are followed
by the mountain cat's paw
There are no maps of this place

I am simply another animal

I enter a clearing
It is shaped like an open hand

THE VORTEX

Within the dream—

the great torrent of the river
with a long walkway out onto the water

I said   there in the narrow gorge
where the water runs fast

we were thrown from our boat
into a waterfall of rapids
were sucked under
then drifted with our craft
half an hour   half a mile
the blackwater penetrating
all but our bellies

before we hugged the shore
crawling up the mudslick bank
bodies shaking for heat

and that night
we would not allow sleep an entrance
holding back until dawn
that deep sucking blackwater swirl

* * *

        and I pointed
to the narrow throat   and spoke
of how long we had been on the river
before we were thrown from our boat
        how far we had gone

that we did not hate the blackwater
        that we would go out again

and then   from the boardwalk
I looked back of that little bottleneck
to the big belly of the gulf

and a heaving whirlpool   sucking down
        a hundred ships

THE THIEF

Time was
I went into sinews of the river
Held me there long

Did not rise again
till I knew its song
The call of all birds
the languages of all beasts

And when I rose up
saw beautiful swan women
and fair maids who swam always
and sang

I wished to go down
to their green caves
Forever

* * *

But no, it was time for Raven
to go travelling
Make my legend great

Many deeds were in that time
for me
And some foolish things
in my name too

* * *

Time was, when Lightning person
struck me
Splitting even the rock under me
but I stood firm

So much had I grown
that even he of Lightning
could not harm

I grew boastful

* * *

I went to the mountain of crystal
and high over
to the great door

into the land of the Sky folk
and beyond to where

House of Sun stood

Such a bright house
I try to steal

And this was the time
I brought his house down
and broke it up

and burned away all the earth
Scorched me black

Better luck next time
the Sky folk say

And laugh me out of the Heaven Door

THE RIVER CHILD

Born on the mountain
snow and black rock
Born on the mountain
in the alder hell

Through brake of buckthorn, hawthorn
and the ninebark tree
O follow O follow O follow me

I am riverwater, listen to my song
I am riverwater, I am strong
I am riverwater, O follow me

Through brake of buckthorn, hawthorn
and the ninebark tree

THE DREAMER

In my sixth year
a diesel locomotive came
and blasted our wood-frame house down
each night

And I lay
sheet over my face
holding my breath

For I took sleep
to be as death
with no breath in it

a dark place
where real life goes
out of you

Yet to that black room
came shaggy-headed cats
huge and hungry
to shake me to life

In daylight
I denied all:

the black room was an empty place

It was not until my twelfth year
that I learned
each night was not death

It was then the woman came
entered my room
and would not leave

Gift I could not return
        could not deny

THE MAGUS

Once was a madman
Chose a child for his confession
Told me his terrible visions

Worst of all was
The Eye

It was huge
and hung in the air
like a hawk

GHOSTS

Forty winters Maquinna ruled
broke the back of the gunship masters
Killed all the Boston men
Had the wolf's wit and the wolf's mercy
grim king, strong hand
Foreseeing downfall and sorrow

* * *

Came the days of pestilence
On all sides men fell dead
The best and the worst together
Children as well
Ruined villages, fallen totems
Where they might have stood to fight
was only the wind

* * *

Of myself, I shall only say
that I took the wanderer's way
Though of my sorrow I have nothing
I would compare

I could not forget you
rising out of that dark lake
Your arm a bright sword
Water clinging to your nakedness

O my love, the razor cut me less

THE HIEROPHANT

As a child in the woodland I saw a mountain
like a bearded man's head. Lake like an eagle
outspread—islet for his eye. But something
tugged. Land was not man or beast, man not land.
But all were here together, and there was a place
they touched.

These serpents are cut deep in the stone.
The great shapes—perhaps dragons—curling
out of a distant age.

What do we know? The war canoes landed on the
beach in the dead of night. The faces of the
warriors were blacked. They crept into the
sleeping village and without a sound cut the
throats of every second man and woman.

We take what we need from the land, but so much
is hidden and wisdom comes late or never.
Thinking of the wooden walls I say this or that
man was wise, but why should it matter if by
chance a man discovers a ring in the belly
of a fish.

GENESIS

Before Raven there was nothing much
It was quite dark

There was no mountain. There was no earth.
There was no sun or fish. There was
no dog or rainbow. There was no
noisy bird or tree. There
was no wind, stone or
rain. There was no
people or
bugs.

It was pretty damn quiet
I am telling you
I was bored

* * *

Then I did something—which
I'm not going to tell

Anyway, after that
Then there are *things*

Like the ocean, for instance
Like the earth-etcetera, for instance

And still later, there was
You—that is, humans, for instance

I make lots of other mistakes too
But at least I was not bored anymore

Which is better than nothing
As they say
And I think I know nothing
well enough to say
it also

THE DROWNED QUEEN

Come, she said

I will harness for you a chariot
of lapis lazuli and of gold
with wheels also of gold and horns of copper
and you shall have storm demons for horses
When you enter our house
it will fill with the fragrance of cedar wood
Threshold and throne will kiss your feet
Kings and princes will bow down before you
They shall bring tribute from mountain and plain

* * *

She entered our lives
on the twelfth night
when the band stopped playing on the upper deck
It was the moment her neck snapped
when she hit the calm breathing of the sea

Passengers, dancers, moved to the rail
as the great ship stopped
as the small boats dropped from the sides

And circling in the tow of the current
in that warm sea
She became electric with phosphorous

She passed the ship's watchers three times
her body glowing

while the searchers, away from the ship
were voices, and a wooden knocking

* * *

It was morning when they reached her:
dark thing in a bright sea

But in the long passage of that night
in each of those thousand watchers
she glowed—as she glows now

watch her pass by

ENVOY

Dark road, dark dream
Raven is travelling
Dark wood, black sky
Raven is travelling

Beak is an axe
Tongue is a flame

Raven is travelling
Is travelling
Home

Book Three

The Axemen

A VISION

Out of the sun in slow circles
Widewinged Shakishak, the hawk, glides
Wings like spread hands held against the sky
Shakishak hunts the sunbright land

    And this is how it can begin:

    Working men silhouetted against the risen sun
    Like dancers lifting the steel bite of heavy boots
    From log to log with rapid step and leap
    Or balancing, walk a long pole
    Cross the plunge of a deep ravine

A kind of ballet
A kind of circus act

This is how it can begin

CHAINSAW

I was up above Jasper Creek
fallin a stand of big rotten cedars
—you know how cedars swell
at the butt and spread out their roots
Well these was like that: real big
and hollow, like wood caves

It was first thing in the mornin
I starts up the chain saw
and lets her roar into the wood
makin it bite deep to break through the shell, ya know
and then it goes into soft stuff
      I figure it's just rot
but then the saw jerks back hard
Starts chokin
and throwin up blood and meat with the cedar chips
      Scared the christ outa me!

Anyhow that's how I killed that she-bear
She was holed up inside one of them damn cedars

I pulled the saw back
and sees the damn thing is smokin
with all this red blood runnin down the blade

THE SPAR TREE

Highclimbing the tall spruce spar

Ninety feet from the earth
I climb to notch and cut
this long tree top

A certain technique, style
I ease up—learn not to grip
life so dear

* * *

Leather strapping
Rhythm of steel spurs
Loop and throw of rope

Glinting blades spring
from ankles like bright wings

carry me out of this day's work
above the long valley, toward the sun

I sway in the wind

* * *

On the ground, lunch break
we sit back and eat
I pick a red salamander
from the woodchips about a notched stump
Slowly it winds its way from my hands

Stacked against the tree—
chains, shackles, blocks,
axes, long guylines
and coils of strawline
They wait: this afternoon's work

The Old Highrigger, my teacher, talks
of those who set up the steam machines
The old-time Skidder Men, his tough masters,
who would climb two hundred feet
then turn about and piss on the crew below

He points down to the valley floor
to a long dead snag, a broken spar,
where one he knew was hit by lightning
and hurled that long fantastic way to earth

We are in the sun and warmth
but look another way down
from our mountain setting
to where the rainclouds press the far Cowichan shore

We stand and stretch
                    and turn to our work

CEDAR

Splitting puncheon
for bridgework

red cedar
bucked seven foot lengths
fine-grained, no limbs

sharp blows ring in the timber
splitting the growth rings
and the spiral of time

sledging wedges down
the long fibre

clean as broken stone

    Nearby the slopes of the Nitinat
    and a stand of cedar bark stripped
    others there stone axes
    fell and split centuries before

red cedar: shakes and planks
yellow cedar: poles and a long canoe
    half-carved, abandoned
    a living tree piercing the hollowed shell

THE GARDEN

Rain slows to fine spray
and we sit, rest in smokebreak calm
Yellow slicker rainclothes, steel helmets
We look out through dreamlike cloud
twisting, churning with the breathing valley winds
The far slopes fade and clear
like the memory of some wild, terrible garden
There is a widespread quiltwork of evergreen
forest, fallen timber, burnt off land, and new growth
And we see how we are connected by these blue arteries—
the winding switchbacks and deadend workroads

Directly across the valley
a yellow spar tower mirrors our own
Stretches out its steel lines over the leveled forest
A steep sidehill that rigging men climb
There is no illusion
We see where these roads lead and where they end
We know these men; we feel the rhythm of their work

The whistle blast of our machine
We rise to our feet
Lift saw or axe and coiled lines
Like men at war—together and alone
we climb the mountain

FIRE IN NOVEMBER

First of November—hot as any summer day

Sun beating out the machine pace of our work
We drag out lines
Choke deadweight hemlock
Skid the long sidehills
Swearing against the sweat, the dirt

More smoke in the valley
Another slash fire broke loose at Renfrew
Forestry crews gone down to help
Two weeks ago there was snow

* * *

After a shower and the cookhouse dinner

I sit on the Cowichan's cool rocky shore

    pick a few smooth red berries
    taste the sour skin, the sweet pulp

and watch the still silver lake

I thought of this all day
But now I think of our contrary nature
Cold water on a hot day. Fire and ice.
And how we live in this forest of work and men,
yet like the Assassins dream of idleness and women

ROADBUILDER'S DREAM

Timbers of this tall
house remember how it is
to sway in the wind

Now I am rocked
to a dark country of sleep
Storm blasting away the night

* * *

I would speak with you
who beckoned me to come to you
on the edge of this road
I built into the wood
on the edge of the dark wood

It was near dusk and I worked late
and you a fair-skinned woman
with raven hair
called me down from my machine
to the dangerous earth

and from the bunched clump
of devil's club and salal
leapt the wolf—
   jaws, white teeth snapping
tearing the thick plaid shirt
from shoulder and arm
and taking some blood as it passed
as I turned, as I rolled away

   and raising a broad axe
sliced his chest
broke his spine
before he could leap again

For you I sliced him
broke him
For you this battle
with the gentle wolf

For you it leapt
for you I killed
I sliced him open
my heart will not rest

In the dark wood
his mate is searching
calling in the night
calling

For you
Lady of the raven hair
skin like a leper
skin like the dead

GIFTS

today from Joe
potlatched me two of his wife's fine cedar baskets
and a story his uncle told him 30 years ago:

He had a weir trap
up the Black Creek
and in mid-winter
went to check it

Found a naked woman
bathing in a pool
crept closer
& she joined by six others
white women all naked
all bathing in the cold winter pool

He stood up
stepped out
to speak with them
but they jumped
from the pool and ran
some taking their clothes
thrown over bushes on the high bank

& when he saw this he understood
they were fur suits, one piece:

these women were bears.

Chased these, one of the young sows
but couldn't catch
went back took her skin
found a slit between hairy legs—
this was what he wanted

on the beach & under bear stare
(looking to see no one about)
went down on the Chetwoot, the She-Bear, the Blackbear
went down on the emptied skin
& through the slit
& through again—to the gravel stone

Nearly crippled himself
walked crab-legged and sore
nearly 3 weeks.

THE VALLEY

A long walk has brought me here
A place that was once a forest's heart
Now a barren logged off flatland

'Real boneyard up there,' he said.

Bleached bones on red earth
I can almost hear hooves clattering
along the dry riverbed
to the deadend gorge wall
where the hunters slaughtered them

'Bones don't lie,' he had said, 'you'll see.'

There are elk antlers larger than any
I had ever known
   bones stacked and scattered everywhere
—many cracked open by wolf jaws
(now even those wolves are gone)
      And then too, the other white bone
of high stumps and bleached deadwood
Bones of a forest
tangled with the small green serpent-life
of creeper and berry vine

I look upon the big bones and scattered ribs
but mostly these long skulls and the great antlers
that fork from the dry earth
like the oak tree in winter
or like a pair of images
growing and caught in that moment
before they form a single
terrible thought

I remain as you, my father
knowing 'bones don't lie'
but unable to truly learn
what they would say
on the land that you have cleared

on the land where your bones are laid

BLOOD BROTHERS

That one was George's idea

Ray was off work with three broke ribs
And as per usual George wasn't working

They was sitting in the Riverside pub
and was both drunk
George got that idea

Ray told him it was bullshit
—only was done for movies
Sides Ray didn't even like George that much anyway
(& maybe heard about that night with his wife)

    Anyways, George keeps on
till Ray finally says OK and
takes out his skinning knife:
    he squints & twists up his mouth
    puts a quarter inch nick on his own finger
    Then takes George's arm
    lays it between the six beerglasses
    & draws a thin line
    from the point of George's finger
    to the inside of his elbow

    and touches the finger nick to it
    Says 'There' & picks up a beer

It don't seem to come to George right away
He just sits there and watches it
Then it opens wide and red like a mouth
And George turns to a real white man
    Didn't say nothin
Just slid real slow to the floor under the table

THE WHITE RAVEN

Snow fills Monday's dawn
landscape—circle of white earth
edged with the black forest

New fallen snow:
this so changes the ruined land
the clean geometry of destruction

And in the centre
the tall spar tree casting
a long shaft of dark shadow

* * *

On such days—when new snow falls
the Cowichans say the white raven rises
from the snowdrift
and the black raven is born
Shadow of that invisibly white bird

I remember doing rough work in deep cold snow
I caught something on the edge of my vision
white, flying up
and heard in that moment
the whistling cry of a bird
I did not know
a sound
that cut like the keen
edge of an axe

and following this (in ugly parody)
a coarse cry that made me turn
to a black raven flattened on the snow
huge and black beaked
cawing and stumbling forward, and finally upward
climbing the air

Later that day, I receive letters from home
and learn that one close friend has died

* * *

So now, the raven is to me
the dark shadow of some man's white soul

and like one who has brought bad news
he is himself abused, despised
and with wide black wings glides
through the pillared cathedral
of this vast deep forest
where all ravens are
robber birds and murderers
who live on looted eggs and stolen fledglings

I know this as surely as
I know all men love the black earth
and ravens are born in winter

FROZEN EARTH

Frozen earth and winds at fifty knots

Boot iron can't bite the wood
We slip and the falls are hard
Real shortage of men. Skeleton crew

    Norcross spoke of a young girl,
    his neighbour, who won the Irish Sweeps
    Nice, good looking girl, he says
    Went to Hawaii for the winter

Eyes and lips sting
A driving wind and cold
that burns the skin

We consider
    the tropical sun, the golden beach
    and no less
    that girl's yielding, pliant body

DAY'S END

Black clouds all day

It is dark by four
      we end it here in wet, cold clothes
travel the forest roads
lights on, our vision poor
—as it was when we came out
in the pre-dawn flooding of whitewater

now in the bus
in this long benched tunnel
the engine drones, dark silhouettes: we are
silent. our cigarettes glow.

STORM

Roots torn from the earth

Windfall stump:

        the tentacle reaching out
and grasping
to anchor deep earth

not this raving in bodiless air
with bluestones like eyes
held upward in black twisting

* * *

Again the onslaught of drenching rain

Under this black sun

the wreckage of a forest

We are slogging against the cold
but it is going badly:
the lines burn, chokers break
the log count is poor

and late in the afternoon
the chaser holds up a broken hand
                bright blood coming down
                the white flesh of his arm

                his slow scream
                lost in the diesel roar

ABLUTION

Curled over, naked

squatting on worn woodslats of the shower stall
with the big bones of leg and trunk bunched
& held with gathering arms

the body is beaten with a down driven
waterfall of heat

half an hour here
driving cold from bone
& the taut cables of muscle
in thighs and arms
slacken and ease

I stagger from the stall
stupid and heavy with heat

ROUTINE

Sitting on my cot
looking at my socks

    Work all day
    Sleep all night

    Go out on weekends
    Drink and fight

* * *

Skies steady and low
Rain comes in swift sheets, then slow
No let up in sight

CAMP LIFE

Hankin took that Vancouver street girl
to the Powell River camp
Kept her three weeks
Then sold her for a hundred dollars

She got passed round
And finally came to the bunkhouse men
Who were with her one night so drunk
Five of them in a clearing behind the camp
Stripped and dragged her down
in one inch of November snow

While she made a dark angel
in the white winter field

BORDERLAND

A cold snap has sealed the earth

    frost and snow crystal
    bright as ground glass

    The sharp odour of broken spruce
as I cross the cleared stumpland

Across the valley
a raven passes between two white mountains

Last night, there was a dream:
        birth of a water marten
        from the mouth of its dead mother
        I assist and there is sharp pain,
        blood and long gashes in my hand
        the creature in panic,
        until I calm its fear,
        stroke its smooth head.

I move on
(boots crunching the snow crusted earth)
towards a high rockbluff
and the fine crystal of a frozen waterfall

    At the base of the falls
in the snow,

I find what I half expect:

        marten tracks
        leading to the forest's dark edge.

BOOKS BY DAVID DAY

The Cowichan (poems)
Many Voices: Canadian Indian Poetry—editor (poems)
The Burroughs Bestiary (fantasy / non-fiction)
The Tolkien Bestiary (fantasy / non-fiction)
The Scarlet Coat Serial (poems / fiction)
The Doomsday Book of Animals (natural history)
Castles (mythology)
The Emperor's Panda (fiction)
Eco-Wars (ecology)
The Animals Within (poems)

ACKNOWLEDGEMENTS

Poems in 'The Lost' sequence were prizewinners in the poetry category of the C.B.C. national literary competition awards for 1982. They were first broadcast on C.B.C. Radio's arts program, 'Anthology'. Poems in 'The Axemen' sequence were first published by Oolichan Press and Harbour Publishing.

Individual poems appeared in the following magazines and anthologies: *The Malahat Review*, *The Fiddlehead*, *Canadian Fiction Magazine*, *Contemporary Verse* II, *Northward Journal*, *Northern Lights*, *Writ*, *Waves*, *Raincoast Chronicles*, *Monday Magazine*, *Poetry Northwest*, *Karaki*, *Tuatara*, *The Martlet*, *Sound Heritage*, *The Poets of Canada* (Hurtig), *Skookum Wawa: Writing of the Canadian Northwest* (Oxford), *Western Windows: Poetry of British Columbia* (ConCept), *A Government Job At Last: An Anthology of Work Poems* (MacLeod), *The Dreadnaught Anthology* (Dreadnaught), *Vancouver Island Poems* (Soft), *Whale Sound: An Anthology of Poems About Whales and Dolphins* (J.J. Douglas).

Special thanks to Earle Birney, Al Purdy and Dennis Lee. A grateful acknowledgement to the Canada Council.

RECENT TITLES IN THE PENUMBRA PRESS POETRY SERIES

1 J. MICHAEL YATES *Insel: The Queen Charlotte Islands Meditations*

2 MARY WEYMARK GOSS *In Hiding*

3 ELIZABETH KOUHI *Round Trip Home*

4 NEILE GRAHAM *Seven Robins*

5 DEBORAH GODIN *Stranded in Terra*

6 M.T. KELLY *Country You Can't Walk In and Other Poems*

7 BARKER FAIRLEY *Wild Geese and Other Poems*

8 DAVID DAY *The Animals Within*

9 ANN FOX CHANDONNET *Auras Tendrils (Poems of the North)*

10 MICHAEL THORPE *Out of the Storm*

11 JIM FLOSDORF *Temagami*

12 GEORGE JOHNSTON *Ask Again*

The Dedalus Press

Decoding Samara

Patrick Deeley